OEDIPUS REX OR OEDIPUS THE KING

Sophocles

AUTHORED by Robert William
UPDATED AND REVISED by Soman Chainani

COVER DESIGN by Table XI Partners LLC
COVER PHOTO by Olivia Verma and © 2005 GradeSaver, LLC

BOOK DESIGN by Table XI Partners LLC

Published by GradeSaver LLC, www.gradesaver.com

First published in the United States of America by GradeSaver LLC. 2008

ISBN 978-1-60259-126-4

Printed in the United States of America

For other products and additional information please visit
http://www.gradesaver.com

Table of Contents

Table of Contents

Biography of Sophocles (496 BC-406 BC [approx])

As with all ancient writers, we can know little for certain about Sophocles' life: sources are few and far between, and much of the information scholars have reached is the result of probability and good guesswork rather than any biographical fact. Some of the sources directly contradict each other.

Sophocles, usually considered the most accessible of the central triangle of Greek tragedians (the other two being Euripides and Aeschylus), was probably born in or around 496 BC at Colonus, near Athens, the setting of his *Oedipus at Colonos* (see, particularly, the Ode to Colonus in that play at 668ff).

Sources tells us that Sophocles wrote 123 plays in his lifetime, of which we know the titles of 118. Of this huge output of plays (Shakespeare, in comparison, wrote somewhere between 36-39 plays in his lifetime) only seven survive: *Antigone*, *Oedipus Rex* (sometimes also called *Oedipus Tyrannos*, *Oedipus at Colonos*, *Ajax*, *Electra*, *The Women of Trachis*, and *Philoctetes*. The tiny size of this sample (around 6% of Sophocles' total output) should be enough to discourage us from making generalizations about Sophocles' style or development as a writer.

All we know about Sophocles' personality is from Aristophanes' later play *Frogs*, which seems to suggest that Sophocles was extremely good-natured and well-liked. Dionysus, in that play, thinks Euripides a 'scoundrel,' likely to try and escape from hell, but Sophocles, because he was good-natured on earth, is assumed to be good-natured in Hades.

His father, Sophillus, was not an aristocrat but rather a wealthy man, which meant that Sophocles was given an excellent education. The first real glimpse of him in the sources reveal that he was chosen after the defeat of the Persians to lead a boys' choir in singing a paean around the trophy of victory, and further accompany the proceedings on the harp.

Nothing more is known about Sophocles until he first appears as a tragic poet at one of the Athenian Festivals (see *About Greek Theatre*) in 468 BC (indeed, we have clearer records for these festivals than we do for Sophocles' life story). He would then have been about twenty-eight years of age, and was entering his first trilogy against the extremely well-renowned Aeschylus. Supposedly, the excitement at this festival was so high that the ten generals, rather than a jury drawn by lots, were asked to decide the winner. They chose Sophocles.

From that point forward, Sophocles seems to have entered tragedies in the competitions something like once every two years, generally winning first prize. He won either eighteen or twenty-four first places at the City Dionysia, and never placed lower than second – and won several other prizes at the Lenaea. Oedipus Tyrannus, incidently, did not place first: the poet Philocles, on this occasion, won the prize (though it is possible that Philocles was entering using the tragedies of his uncle, Aeschylus, rather than ones he had himself written!). No full trilogy of Sophocles' survives: the so-called 'Theban Plays', of which Oedipus Tyrannus is one, is not actually a full trilogy, and were not written in the order of their story, across Sophocles' lifetime (Antigone comes first, Oedipus Tyrannus in his old age, and Oedipus at Colonos is only produced after Sophocles' death).

Sophocles is famously supposed by Aristotle in the *Poetics* to have added the third speaking actor to the Greek stage (probably sometime around 460: Aeschylus' *Oresteia* [which requires three actors] follows two years later in 458 BC. Sophocles also supposedly increased the chorus size, even writing a treatise on the use of the chorus within the plays (which has not survived).

The bond between Greek theatre and Greek society is also evident in Sophocles' career. He was a senior administrator in the Athenian Empire, and elected to become one of the ten generals in charge of the military. He is also credited with introducing the cult of the healing god Asclepius into Athens: a result, perhaps, of the great plague that struck in the early years of the Peloponnesian War.

For many years, a long tradition of criticism held Sophocles above both Aeschylus and Euripides, hailing his work as the apex of Greek tragedy. This conclusion, it might be said, has undergone considerable revision, and any such value judgment would today be shot down by classical scholars. That said, Aristotle praised him above all other playwrights, using *Oedipus the King* as a model for the perfect tragedy in his highly influential *Poetics.*

Sophocles continued to write and serve in government well into his eighties. He died in c.406 BC. And yet, despite leaving us only a small sample of seven complete plays, Sophocles still left a legacy powerful enough to make him one of the founding fathers of Western drama.

About Oedipus Rex or Oedipus the King

The Oedipus myth goes back as far as Homer and beyond, with sources varying about plot details. The play that Sophocles presents is merely the end of a dramatically long story, and some plot background must be provided to make the story understandable for modern audiences (please see the section on 'Oedipus and Myth' for this full backstory). The real myth begins a few generations before Oedipus was born. The city of Thebes was founded by a man named Cadmus, who slew a dragon and was instructed to sow the dragon's teeth in order to give birth to a city. From these teeth sprang a race of giants who were fully armed and angry; they fought each other until only five were left, and these five became the fathers of Thebes.

Ancient Greek audiences would already know the background, and in fact the entirety, of the Oedipus story. Therefore what makes this particular play so great is its ability to present this material in an evocative and powerful manner, in order to nullify the reality that most of the audience already knew its contents. Modern audiences might recognize the name Oedipus from Sigmund Freud's famous "Oedipus Complex" - particularly his theory that young boys lust after their mothers and see their fathers as competition for their mothers' favors. This theory springs from Jocasta's comment that killing your father and marrying your mother are the kinds of things men often dream of (981). Freud's theory has been hotly debated and, indeed, is currently dismissed by most classical scholars – though the fact that the issue remains the subject of much psychological debate is proof that the Oedipus story continues to be powerful even thousands of years after the advent of Sophocles' play.

Character List

Oedipus

Oedipus is the king of Thebes, married to Jocasta. He is unaware, at the start of the play, that he has murdered his father and slept with his mother. Soon he learns that it was he that put his kingdom at such terrible risk, and blinds himself using a brooch. He has a 'tell-tale limp', a piercing wound in his ankles, made as a child by the father who exposed him. This echoes his name, which roughly translates as 'swollen-feet'. In line with most tragic 'heroes,' Oedipus has a clear hamartia - or tragic flaw - which precipitates his woeful fate. in this case, it's his pride, which allows him to disbelieve the Gods and hunt the source of a plague instead of looking inside himself. That said, Oedipus' hamartia is not always so clear - since it appears that his prideful sins occurred long before the start of the play. Indeed, Oedipus' greatest sin appears to take place when he kills a man at a roadside in a fit of temper, suggesting that no deed goes unpunished. Ultimately, however, Oedipus must pay the price for dismissing Teiresias' judgment and the Oracle's prophecy, as yet another reminder that the Gods are infinitely more powerful than men.

Jocasta

Jocasta is the wife and mother of Oedipus and queen of Thebes. Before marrying Oedipus, she was married to Laius. She commits suicide at the end of the play, perhaps in guilt that she left Oedipus to die as a baby, thus precipitating his course towards a tragic end for their whole family.

Teiresias

Teiresias is the blind prophet, led by a small boy, who knows the truth about Oedipus's parentage. Oedipus calls on him to find Laius's killer but becomes furious when Teiresias claims that Oedipus himself is the killer. Teiresias's words, however, prove true ultimately, suggesting that he is a mouthpiece for the Gods and an oracle to be trusted far more than the convictions and hopes of man. Teiresias is often represented as being part-male, part-female in classical literature.

Creon

Creon is Jocasta's brother, who shares one third of Thebes's riches with Oedipus and Jocasta. He is a devout follower of the oracle of Apollo, and as the play opens, he is returning from the oracle with the news that Laius's killer must be found. He is a loyal friend to Oedipus, and ultimately remains forgiving and kind to Oedipus even when Oedipus turns on him and suggests he is conspiring against him. He is to take over Thebes after Oedipus' exile. (Creon also takes center stage in Sophocles' play, Antigone, which adds another chapter to Oedipus' doomed lineage.)

Messenger from Corinth

The Messenger from Corinth arrives to tell Oedipus that his father, Polybus, is dead, and that the people of Corinth wish Oedipus to be their new king. He also reveals to Oedipus, however, that Polybus and Meropé are not his real parents. He says that long ago a stranger from Thebes gave him a baby as a gift to the king and queen of Corinth. This baby was, of course, Oedipus who would grow up to be king himself. The Messenger, then, provides the audience with the first real clue of dramatic irony that suggests that Teiresias' words (and those of the Oracle) are true - long before Oedipus discovers their veracity.

Herdsman

The Herdsman gives Laius' and Jocasta's baby to the messenger upon their orders - and is also the same man who witnessed Laius's death. When he returns to Thebes and sees that the man who killed Laius is the new king, he asks leave to flee from the city. Oedipus sends for him when the messenger alludes to his intimate knowledge of the crime, in the hopes of discovering the identity of his true parents. He then reveals that the baby he gave to the messenger was Laius and Jocasta's son, adding one of the last pieces to the puzzle that will implicate Oedipus as the source of the kingdom's plague.

Priest

The Priest's followers make sacrifices to the gods at the beginning of the play, hoping that the gods will lift the plague that has struck the city. At this point, the followers believe that the Gods have punished the city for some sin that must be rooted out. Oedipus, then, takes it upon himself to visit the Oracle to determine whose sin it is and for how it might be atoned.

Second Messenger

The Second Messenger is a servant of Oedipus and Jocasta who tells Oedipus and the Chorus of Jocasta's suicide.

Ismene and Antigone

Ismene and Antigone are Oedipus's young daughters who are led out at the end of the play. Oedipus laments the fact that they will never find husbands with such a cursed lineage and begs Creon to take care of them. Antigone, in the *Oedipus at Colonus*, will become her father's guide.

Chorus of Theban Elders

The Chorus of Theban Elders is a group of men who serve as an emotional sounding board and expositional device in the play, reflecting on the plot developments while asking important philosophical questions. The Chorus speaks as one person, but occasionally, single Chorus members would have delivered lines. They might be considered somewhat meta-theatrical - operating within the confines of the play while also having the power to step outside the boundaries of the mundane plot.

Major Themes

Light and darkness

Darkness and light are tightly wound up with the theme of sight and blindness in Sophocles' play. Oedipus - and all the other characters, save for Teiresias - is 'in the dark' about his own origins and the murder of Laius. Teiresias, of course, is literally 'in the dark' with his own blindness - and yet manages to have sight over everything that is to follow. After Oedipus finds out what has happened, he bemoans the way everything has indeed "come to light".

Sight and blindness

Teiresias holds the key to the link between sight and blindness - for even though he is blind, he can still see and predict the future (if not the present). At the end of the play, moreover, Oedipus blinds himself, because what he has metaphorically seen (i.e. realized) leaves him unable to face his family or his parents in the afterlife). As with the previous theme, sight/blindness operate both literally and metaphorically within the play. Indeed, literal sight is juxtaposed with 'insight' or 'foresight'.

Origins and children

Oedipus embarks upon a search for his own origins, and - though he does not realize it - for his real parents. As the child of his own wife, and thus father and brother to his children, Sophocles explores various interrelationships between where things began and who fathered who. Similarly, the play itself works backwards towards a revelatory start: the story has, in effect, already happened - and Oedipus is forced to discover his own history.

The one and the many (also doubles/twos)

Throughout the play, a central inconsistency dominates - namely the herdsman and Jocasta both believe Laius to have been killed by several people at the crossroads. The story, however, reveals that Oedipus himself alone killed Laius. How can Laius have been supposedly killed by one person – and also by many people?

Oedipus is searching for Laius' murderer: he is the detective seeking the criminal. Yet in the end, these two roles merge into one person – Oedipus himself. The Oedipus we are left with at the end of the play is similarly both father and brother. Sophocles' play, in fact, abounds with twos and doubles: there are two herdsmen, two brothers (Oedipus and Creon), two daughters and two sons, two opposed pairs of king and queen (Laius and Jocasta, and Polybus and Merope), and two cities (Thebes and Corinth). In so many of these cases, Oedipus' realization is that he is either between – or, more confusingly, some combination of – two things. Thus the conflict between "the one and the many" is central to Sophocles' play. "What is this news of double meaning?" Jocasta asks (939). Throughout Oedipus, then, it remains a pertinent question.

Plague and health

Thebes at the start of the play is suffering from terrible blight which renders the fields and the women barren. The oracle tells Oedipus at the start of the play that the source of this plague is Laius' murderer (Oedipus himself). Health then, only comes with the end of the play and Oedipus' blindness. Again, 'plague' is both literal and metaphorical. There is a genuine plague, but also, to quote Hamlet, there might be "something rotten" in the moral state of Thebes.

Prophecy, oracles, and predestination

The origins of this play in the Oedipus myth (see 'Oedipus and Myth') create an compelling question about foreknowledge and expectation. The audience who knew the myth would know from the start far more than Oedipus himself - hence a strong example of dramatic irony. Moreover, one of the themes the play considers as a corollary is whether or not you can escape your fate. In trying to murder her son, Jocasta finds him reborn as her husband. Running from Corinth, from his parents, Oedipus murders his father on the way. It seems that running away from one's fate ultimately ensures that one is only running towards it.

Youth and age

'Man' is the answer to the Sphinx's question, and the aging of man is given key significance in the course of the play. Oedipus himself goes from childlike innocence to a blinded man who needs to be led by his children. Oedipus, it might be said, ages with the discovery of his own shortcomings as a man. In learning of his own weaknesses and frailties, he loses his innocence immediately.

Glossary of Terms

agon

Agon is the Greek word for 'conflict.'

City Dionysia

Dionysia is a festival held in Athens, which includes a tragedy competition. (See 'About Greek Theater' for more information).

dramatic irony

Dramatic irony is a situation in which the characters on stage do not know something (or some of them do not know something) which the audience does know. Dramatic irony recurs throughout Oedipus - for instance, when the Messenger suggests that he never killed the young baby that Jocasta had given him, signifying that he clearly had grown up to become Oedipus the King. Oedipus, however, does not realize this until much later.

oikos

Oikos is the greek word for 'household' or 'house' - often used to mean 'bloodline' or 'family'. It is the opposite to 'polis'.

polis

Polis is usually translated to 'city-state', but as well as literally referring to the city, it can also be the Greek word for 'citizenship', or 'body of citizens'.

satyr play

The satyr play is the fourth, probably comic, play that would have been performed after a trilogy and written by the same author. The only surviving satyr play is Euripides' *Cyclops*.

skene

A skene is the permanent stone building at the back of the stage in which costumes and props could be stored, and which served variously as the internal locations that the play might require (houses, tents, etc.).

Thebes

Thebes is city in which the play is set and is often set up in classical literature as the 'other' or 'opposite' to Athens, where the City Dionysia took place.

Short Summary

When the play opens, Thebes is suffering a plague which leaves its fields and women barren. Oedipus, the king of Thebes, has sent his brother-in-law, Creon, to the house of Apollo to ask the oracle how to end the plague. Creon returns, bearing good news: once the killer of the previous king, Laius, is found, Thebes will be cured of the plague (Laius was Jocasta's husband before she married Oedipus). Hearing this, Oedipus swears he will find the murderer and banish him. The Chorus (representing the people of Thebes) suggests that Oedipus consult Teiresias, the blind prophet. Oedipus tells them that he has already sent for Teiresias.

When Teiresias arrives, he seems reluctant to answer Oedipus's questions, warning him that he does not want to know the answers. Oedipus threatens him with death, and finally Teiresias tells him that Oedipus himself is the killer, and that his marriage is a sinful union. Oedipus takes this as an insult and jumps to the conclusion that Creon paid Teiresias to say these things. Furious, Oedipus dismisses him, and Teiresias goes, repeating as he does, that Laius's killer is right here before him - – a man who is his father's killer and his mother's husband, a man who came seeing but will leave in blindness.

Creon enters, asking the people around him if it is true that Oedipus slanderously accused him. The Chorus tries to mediate, but Oedipus appears and charges Creon with treason. Jocasta and the Chorus beg Oedipus to be open-minded: Oedipus unwillingly relents and allows Creon to go. Jocasta asks Oedipus why he is so upset and he tells her what Teiresias prophesied. Jocasta comforts him by telling him that there is no truth in oracles or prophets, and she has proof. Long ago an oracle told Laius that his own son would kill him, and as a result he and Jocasta gave their infant son to a shepherd to leave out on a hillside to die with a pin through its ankles. Yet Laius was killed by robbers, not by his own son, proof that the oracle was wrong. But something about her story troubles Oedipus; she said that Laius was killed at a place where three roads meet, and this reminds Oedipus of an incident from his past, when he killed a stranger at a place where three roads met. He asks her to describe Laius, and her description matches his memory. Yet Jocasta tells him that the only eyewitness to Laius's death, a herdsman, swore that five robbers killed him. Oedipus summons this witness.

While they wait for the man to arrive, Jocasta asks Oedipus why he seems so troubled. Oedipus tells her the story of his past. Once when he was young, a man he met told him that he was not his father's son. He asked his parents about it, and they denied it. Still it troubled him, and he eventually went to an oracle to determine his true lineage. The oracle then told him that he would kill his father and marry his mother. This prophecy so frightened Oedipus that he left his hometown and never returned. On his journey, he encountered a haughty man at a crossroads - and killed the man after suffering an insult. Oedipus is afraid that the stranger he killed might have been Laius. If this is the case, Oedipus will be forever banished both from

Thebes (the punishment he swore for the killer of Laius) and from Corinth, his hometown. If this eyewitness will swear that robbers killed Laius, then Oedipus is exonerated. He prays for the witness to deliver him from guilt and from banishment. Oedipus and Jocasta enter the palace to wait for him.

Jocasta comes back out of the palace, on her way to the holy temples to pray for Oedipus. A messenger arrives from Corinth with the news that Oedipus's father Polybus is dead. Overjoyed, Jocasta sends for Oedipus, glad that she has even more proof in the uselessness of oracles. Oedipus rejoices, but then states that he is still afraid of the rest of the oracle's prophecy: that he will marry his mother. The messenger assures him that he need not fear approaching Corinth - since Merope, his mother, is not really his mother, and moreover, Polybus wasn't his father either. Stunned, Oedipus asks him how he came to know this. The messenger replies that years ago a man gave a baby to him and he delivered this baby to the king and queen of Corinth - a baby that would grow up to be Oedipus the King. The injury to Oedipus's ankles is a testament to the truth of his tale, because the baby's feet had been pierced through the ankles. Oedipus asks the messenger who gave the baby to him, and he replies that it was one of Laius's servants. Oedipus sends his men out to find this servant. The messenger suggests that Jocasta should be able to help identify the servant and help unveil the true story of Oedipus's birth. Suddenly understanding the terrible truth, Jocasta begs Oedipus not to carry through with his investigation. Oedipus replies that he swore to unravel this mystery, and he will follow through on his word. Jocasta exits into the palace.

Oedipus again swears that he will figure out this secret, no matter how vile the answer is. The Chorus senses that something bad is about to happen and join Jocasta's cry in begging the mystery to be left unresolved. Oedipus's men lead in an old shepherd, who is afraid to answer Oedipus's questions. But finally he tells Oedipus the truth. He did in fact give the messenger a baby boy, and that baby boy was Laius's son - the same son that Jocasta and Laius left on a hillside to die because of the oracle's prophecy.

Finally the truth is clear - devastated, Oedipus exits into the palace. A messenger reveals that he grabbed a sword and searched for Jocasta with the intent to kill her. Upon entering her chamber, however, he finds that she has hanged herself. He takes the gold brooches from her dress and gouges his eyes out. He appears onstage again, blood streaming from his now blind eyes. He cries out that he, who has seen and done such vile things, shall never see again. He begs the Chorus to kill him. Creon enters, having heard the entire story, and begs Oedipus to come inside, where he will not be seen. Oedipus begs him to let him leave the city, and Creon tells him that he must consult Apollo first. Oedipus tells him that banishment was the punishment he declared for Laius's killer, and Creon agrees with him. Before he leaves forever, however, Oedipus asks to see his daughters and begs Creon to take care of them. Oedipus is then led away, while Creon and the girls go back in the palace. The Chorus, alone, laments Oedipus' tragic fate and his doomed lineage.

Summary and Analysis of Prologue, Parode and First Episode (1-462)

The play opens in front of Oedipus' palace at Thebes. A plague besets the city, and Oedipus enters to find a priest and crowd of children praying to the gods to free them from the curse. A blight, the priest tells Oedipus, has destroyed their crops and livestock - and even rendered their women sterile, unable to have children. The priest implores Oedipus to save the city: "Raise up our city, save it and raise it up" (51). Oedipus tells the collected crowd that even though he knows they are sick, none is as sick and devastated as he: thus clearly identifying himself with Thebes.

Oedipus tells the priest that he has sent Creon to the temple of Apollo to glean from the gods how the city might be saved. Creon then arrives and announces the command from the Oracle: "Drive out a pollution…. Grown ingrained within the land" (98-9) - namely the murderer of Laius.

"Where would a trace / of this old crime be found?" Oedipus asks – Laius was murdered many years ago (108-9). Creon speaks with a messenger who fled in terror from the roadside where Laius was killed. This messenger, in turn, reveals that

…the robbers they encountered
were many and the hands that did the murder
were many; it was no man's single power.
(123-5)

Oedipus swears to solve the murder, both as part of his duty as king as well as for the good of the city: 'So helping the dead king I help myself' (141). All soon exit, save for the chorus. The chorus of children pray to the gods Apollo, Athene, Artemis and Phoebus in the Parode, compare the city of Thebes to a ship whose "timbers are rotten" (169), and beg for help lifting the curse.

Oedipus returns, reiterates his commitment to tracking down the murderer, and commands that anyone who knows the murderer must speak out. He then invokes a curse upon the murderer – "may he wear out his life / in misery to miserable doom" (249). The Chorus advises him to seek Teiresias, a seer, who might be able to better see the purposes of the gods.

Teiresias arrives, led by a little boy, and Oedipus asks him to name the murderer. Teiresias initially refuses, and attempts to leave; Oedipus responds angrily, and Teiresias tells him that even his words "miss the mark" (325). "All of you here know nothing," Teiresias says, and Oedipus furiously accuses Teiresias himself of being "complotter of the deed" with Creon (348). Teiresias tells Oedipus that Oedipus himself is Thebes' pollution.

Oedipus rejects Teiresias' words, and calls him "blind in mind and ears / as well as in your eyes" (371-2) – Teiresias responds simply that these are insults which everyone will soon heap upon Oedipus himself. Oedipus, now suspicious of Creon as a conspirator with Teiresias, outlines his own achievement in solving the riddle of the sphinx. The Chorus attempts to calm down the escalating anger, but Teiresias makes another long speech: Oedipus, he says, does not know where he is, where he lives, whom his parents are, or even who he is, and prophesies that he will be driven out from the city, "with darkness on your eyes." An argument ensues between Oedipus and Teiresias, in which Teiresias tells him that "in riddle answering you are strongest" (440). Teiresias makes one final prediction: that the murderer will have "blindness for sight" and "beggary for riches", before being proved both "father and brother" to the children in his house. He and Oedipus exit, leaving the Chorus alone onstage.

Analysis

The opening of the play treats the murder of Laius as a detective story. Indeed, Oedipus speaks of tracks and traces, and the oracle gives little clue as to the events that will unfold. What Oedipus does as the tragic hero, however, is to speed up this revelation of events. Notable too is the literal plague that affects the city as well as the metaphorical 'pollution' within it: namely Oedipus himself. Indeed, in Athenian culture, the incest which Oedipus has committed - as well as the murder of his father - would have been considered both crimes against the natural order and crimes against the gods. Incest, of course, still carries a weighty taboo in most societies today. Because he fathered a child with his mother, he has engendered a plague on Oedipus' kingdom, Thebes, which has rendered the women sterile.

What is key to remember in analyzing this opening section of the play is the first glimpse Sophocles' gives us of Oedipus' deeper character. Sophocles starts the tragedy when Oedipus' fortune is at its very height – he has solved the riddle and is a prosperous, respected king with wife and children. Note how many times in this early section of the play he is referred to as Oedipus the 'great'. Some commentators have also found in Oedipus an unpleasant arrogance or pride – a sense of self-regard – which might be considered a 'tragic flaw' (an idea that seems to come from a mistranslation of the word *hamartia* meaning 'mistake'). One might also suggest that Oedipus' pride is manifest in his identification of himself with Thebes, the city - and of the way he takes up the challenge of finding the murderer in order to secure his own kingship.

This is a compelling reading, but it is similarly important to remember that, even at this first stage of the play, Oedipus' pride does not bring about any of the events that cause the plague. The murder of Laius, after all, happened many years ago, and he already has four children fathered by his mother. Though Oedipus' own pride is responsible for his ultimate discovery of what he has done, it does not actually cause it. Oedipus' so-called 'tragic flaw' has surprisingly very little to do with his tragic fate.

The play begins with an idiosyncratic juxtaposition: a chorus of children, against the Chorus of the play itself, comprised of old men from Thebes. This contradiction is later played out in the character of Teiresias, an old man (partially male and partially female in myth) led by a young boy. This immediately raises questions of past and future. These questions are especially important, considering that Sophocles' deliberately begins his play approximately half-way through the Oedipus myth (see 'The Oedipus Myth'). One of the ways in which of Oedipus' unknown past is revealed to shape his future involves a continuation of his tragic lineage - his children turn out to be, in bizarre, self-consuming fashion, the same generation as him.

These revelations lead Oedipus to blind himself, leaving him a helpless old man (led around in the *Oedipus at Colonos* by a child, like Teiresias) exactly in the manner of the riddle of the Sphinx. In one sense, Oedipus ultimately frees himself from blind youth in order to discover painful wisdom. In another sense, Oedipus also goes backward – and realizes he is a child with a mother, as well as a father with a child.

Summary and Analysis of First Stasimon, Second Episode, Second Stasimon and Third Episode (462-1086)

The Chorus wonders who the murderer might be and suggests that now would be time for him to "run / with a stronger foot / than Pegasus" (467-9) as the fates run up "terribly close on his heels" (472). The Chorus also proclaims itself in "terrible confusion", and doesn't understand why Teiresias might have attacked Oedipus' "popular fame" (493). Furthermore, they side with Oedipus, asserting that they would never agree with someone who finds fault with their King, particularly since he solved the riddle of the Sphinx.

Creon enters, having heard the king accused him of wrongdoing. Oedipus enters and further indicts him as the murderer himself, guilty of crafting a plot against him. Creon mocks Oedipus as "obstinacy without wisdom" (549) – but Oedipus replies that his public interest supersedes his private: "you are wrong if you believe that one / a criminal, will not be punished only / because he is my kinsman" (551-3). Oedipus' belief at this stage is that Teiresias is a vicious liar, and as he was sent by Creon, Creon must be involved in the plot against him.

He and Creon argue, and Creon tells him that they searched for information about Laius' death but found none. Creon, moreover, informs Oedipus that he is happy with his life and has no reason to plot against him – and reminds Oedipus in a long speech that since there is no proof against him, Oedipus cannot cast such damaging aspersions until fully supported. Creon then tells him that 'in time you will know all with certainty" (613). Oedipus refuses to listen, and Creon finishes his diatribe by accusing the king of ruling unjustly.

Jocasta enters and berates the two men for airing their private griefs when there is a public crisis. The men repeat their arguments, and she begs Oedipus to believe Creon and to be merciful. The Chorus joins in her pleas, and Oedipus reluctantly lets Creon go. At this stage, each of the brothers think the other is the murderer of Laius.

Jocasta reveals that an oracle once came to Laius and told him that he would be killed by his son, though she too reiterates that Laius "was killed by foreign highway robbers / at a place where three roads meet" (715-6). She tells Oedipus that, three days after his birth, Laius pierced the ankles of the child and had him cast forth "upon a pathless hillside" (720). This news worries Oedipus, for some reason. He asks exactly where the crossroads was that Laius was killed – Jocasta tells him, and describes Laius. "I think I have / called curses on myself in ignorance", says Oedipus (744-5), fearing he has killed his father. They send for the herdsman who escaped from the murder-scene at the crossroads.

Oedipus then tells Jocasta of Polybus and Merope, his father and mother and king and queen of Corinth. A drunken man, he says, accused him of being a bastard at a feast - and he confronted his parents with this to no avail. Eventually he went to an oracle, which did not tell him of his parentage, but warned him he would sleep with his mother and murder his father. Oedipus then fled Corinth, and at a crossroads, fell into an argument with an old man in a coach. Oedipus "struck him backwards from the car" (811) and killed him. Oedipus now fears that he has killed Laius, his father, and married Jocasta, his mother, but waits for the herdsman to arrive. Oedipus hopes that the herdsman will say that many people killed Laius - for he alone killed the man at the crossroads.

The Chorus criticizes pride, but at the same time hopes for the preservation of the "eager ambition that profits the state" (881). Jocasta returns with garlands for the Theban Elders hoping to go to the temple. A messenger enters from Corinth bringing the news that Polybus, King of Corinth, is dead – and that Oedipus has been chosen as the Corinthian king. Jocasta is delighted, for, if Polybus is Oedipus' father, the oracle must be false: he has not died at Oedipus' hands, but rather of sickness. Oedipus reenters, and laughs delightedly, telling the Corinthian messenger of the tragic prophecy he has avoided. The messenger tells Oedipus he had no need to worry: for he was not the son of Polybus and Merope. Rather, it was he - this very messenger - that took the baby from the shepherd, who found him as a baby in the mountains, with his ankles pierced. Oedipus suddenly realizes that the plot has thickened - and he may still be guilty.

Oedipus immediately sends for the shepherd. Jocasta begs him not to "hunt this out", despite the "clues" Oedipus has suddenly uncovered. It is clear that she has realized what has happened, and she exits. The Chorus ask where she has gone, and Oedipus, calling himself a child of Fortune, boldly challenges the heavens: "Break out what will!" (1077).

Analysis

Everyone is still in the dark as to the true nature of the curse on the kingdom. Only Jocasta, who has gone into the house, has suffered the awful realization of the truth, and her immediate response is to commit suicide to absolve herself of guilt. Oedipus' long recounting of past history reveals the way that Sophocles has started his play, effectively halfway through the story - precisely, in fact, at the point of greatest prosperity for his protagonist (a fall from great height – since Aristotle, and carried on via Chaucer in *The Monk's Tale* – is traditionally part of the tragic construction). The story of the play is much like, then, a detective story: for Oedipus must work backwards in time, creating an emphasis in the early part of the play, and now again, on finding clues and following according lines of inquiry. The criminal Oedipus is seeking, however, is himself.

A central inconsistency appears in the play at this point. The herdsman and Jocasta both believe Laius to have been killed by several people at the crossroads: the story, in the end, reveals that Oedipus himself alone killed Laius. How can Laius have been supposedly killed by one person – and also by many people? Some critics, notably Frederick Ahl, in his *Sophocles' Oedipus: Evidence and Self-Contradiction* (Ithaca, 1992), have argued that Oedipus did not in fact kill his father, and is talked into taking responsibility for the crime. This is not a particularly convincing interpretation – and one far more likely presents itself both in the play itself and as a device in Greek tragedy as a whole.

Oedipus is searching for Laius' murderer - and thus is the detective seeking the criminal. Yet in the end, these two roles merge into one person – Oedipus himself. The Oedipus we are left with at the end of the play is similarly both father and brother. Sophocles' play, in fact, abounds with twos and doubles: there are two herdsmen, two brothers (Oedipus and Creon), two daughters and two sons, two opposed pairs of king and queen (Laius and Jocasta, and Polybus and Merope), and two cities (Thebes and Corinth). In so many of these cases, Oedipus' realization is that he is either between – or, more confusingly, some combination of – two things. Thus the conflict between "the one and the many" is central to Sophocles' play. "What is this news of double meaning?" Jocasta asks (939). And indeed, throughout Oedipus, it is a pertinent question.

Yet another of Oedipus' dual roles involves that of king and man. As King of Thebes, as he states at the start of the play, it is his duty to work to rid Thebes from the dreadful plague which blights it, and – as it turns out – this ends up being an unconscious self-sacrifice. Yet Oedipus, by demanding that Creon exile him from Thebes, does remove the plague (himself) from the city. Ultimately, then, his public role is given priority of his private one. This is further evidenced by the death of his wife (and the later death of his two sons, Polyneices and Eteocles) – in exactly the way that Creon's public decision brings about the implosion of his family in Sophocles' *Antigone.*

Yet significantly, Oedipus does free the city of Thebes from the plague exactly as he initially promises. So though the play is a tragedy in the light of Oedipus' demise, there is a possibility that, for any Athenian who was public-minded enough to see the play from Theban perspective, *Oedipus Rex* might in some sense be a play with a happy ending.

Summary and Analysis of Third Stasimon, Fourth Episode, Fourth Stasimon, and Exode (1087 – 1530)

The Chorus wonders aloud about the origins of Oedipus. An old man is led in by Oedipus' servants and identified as the herdsman, the man who gave the baby to the Corinthian messenger so many years ago: Oedipus insists on him revealing exactly what he knows. The messenger says that Oedipus is that same baby, who was abandoned by his father and mother - and the herdsman reacts with fear and begs the messenger to hold his tongue. Oedipus threatens the messenger with physical violence, and finally the man confesses that the baby was a child of Laius's house.

Oedipus asks if it was a slave's child or Laius's child, and the shepherd confesses that it was Laius's child - a child that Jocasta gave him to expose on the hillside because of a prophecy that he would kill his father. The shepherd says he didn't have the heart to kill the infant, so he took it to another country instead. "They will all come, / all come out clearly!" cries Oedipus. "Light of the sun, let me / look on you no more!" (1183-4). He has finally realized what has happened and all exit except the Chorus. The Chorus reflects on the mutable nature of human happiness - all happiness, they say, is only "a seeming" and "after that turning away" (1191-2). Nobody can ultimately escape fate.

A messenger enters from the palace with horrifying news. In a long speech, he says that Jocasta went into the palace, went straight to her bedroom and slammed the door, tearing her hair with her fingers. There she cried out to Laius and bemoaned the tragedy of her son/husband. Oedipus, bursting into the palace and demanding a sword, found that Jocasta had hanged herself. Moaning horribly, he cut her down and laid her on the ground. Then he took the gold brooches with which she had fastened her gown, and, thrusting his arms out at full length, gouged his eyes out. Again and again he pierced he eyes until bloody tears streamed down his cheeks. Now he shouts for someone to open the palace doors (presumably the doors of the skene building) and show all of Thebes the man who killed Laius. He swears he will flee this country to rid his house of his curse.

The doors to the palace are thrown open, and Oedipus stumbles out. The Chorus cries out in agony at the sight and hides its own eyes: "this is", they say, "a terrible sight for men to see" (1298). Oedipus cries out to the city in a voice that hardly seems his own. The Chorus wails that Oedipus is untouchable and too terrible for eyes to see - that he has been punished in both body and soul. Oedipus calls for someone to be his guide. He pleads with the Chorus to lead him out of Thebes and curses the shepherd who saved his life when he was a baby. The Chorus tells him that surely death would have been better than blindness, and Oedipus replies by asking how he could have possibly met his parents in the underworld with seeing eyes. How could he have looked upon children whom he had begotten in sin? He begs the Chorus to hide him away from human sight.

Creon enters, and asks the Chorus to take Oedipus inside: "only kin", he thinks, "should see and hear the troubles / of kin" (1430-1). Oedipus begs to be cast out of Thebes. Creon replies that he must wait for instructions from Apollo. Oedipus argues that Apollo's instructions were clear: the unclean man must leave Thebes. Oedipus also asks Creon to bury Jocasta properly and to take care of his daughters. But before he goes, he begs to see his daughters once more. These girls, Antigone and Ismene are led in, and Oedipus caresses them with hands that are both father's and brother's. He weeps for the fact that they will never be able to find husbands with this tragic family lineage. With Creon's promise that he will send him away from Thebes to fulfill Apollo's word, Oedipus releases his children and he and Creon enter the palace again.

Alone on the stage, the Chorus asks the audience to remember the story of Oedipus, the greatest of men. He alone could solve difficult riddles and was envied my his fellows for his prosperity - but now the greatest of misfortunes has befallen him. The Chorus warns the audience that mortal men must always "look upon that last day always" (1529). Only after life can one be sure that one's life is "secure from pain" (1530).

Analysis

Sophocles' use of dramatic irony takes center stage in the play's third act. Here, the narrative revolves around two different attempts to change the course of fate: Jocasta and Laius's killing of Oedipus at birth and Oedipus's flight from Corinth as an adult. In both cases, an oracle's prophecy comes true regardless of the characters' actions. Jocasta kills her son only to find him restored to life and married to her. Oedipus leaves Corinth only to find that in so doing he has found his real parents and carried out the oracle's words. Both Oedipus and Jocasta prematurely exult over the failure of oracles, only to find that the oracles ultimately proved accurate. Furthermore, each time a character tries to avert a future predicted by the oracles, the audience knows their attempt is futile. As this final Chorus confirms: fate is inescapable.

Even the manner in which Oedipus and Jocasta express their disbelief in oracles proves ironic. In an attempt to comfort Oedipus, Jocasta tells him that oracles are powerless, yet minutes later we see her praying to the same gods whose powers she just mocked (911). Oedipus rejoices over Polybus's death as a sign that oracles are fallible, yet he will not return to Corinth for fear that the oracle's statements concerning Merope could still come true (976). Regardless of what they say, both Jocasta and Oedipus continue to suspect that the oracles could be right, that gods can predict and affect the future. In a way, then, they reflect both the Athenian audience's own ambivalence towards oracles.

Yet, if Oedipus discounts the power of oracles, he values the power of truth. Instead of relying on the gods, Oedipus counts on his own ability to root out the truth -

indeed, the opening of the play posits him as a miraculous riddle-solver. The contrast between trust in the gods' oracles and trust in intelligence plays out in this story much like the contrast between religion and science in nineteenth-century novels. But the irony here, of course, is that the oracles and Oedipus's scientific method both lead to the same outcome. Oedipus's search for truth fulfills the oracles' prophesies. Ironically, it is Oedipus's rejection of the oracles that uncovers their power; he relentlessly pursues truth instead of trusting in the gods. As Jocasta says, if he could just have left well enough alone, he would never have discovered his own awful secret.

In his search for the truth, Oedipus shows himself to be a formidable detective, ruthless in his pursuit of solving the mystery. This persistence is the same characteristic that brought him to Thebes; he was the only man capable of solving the Sphinx's riddle. His intelligence is what makes him great, and yet also proves his tragic flaw. Indeed, his problem-solver's mind leads him closer and closer to tragedy as he works through the mystery of his birth. In the Oedipus myth, marriage to Jocasta was the prize for ridding Thebes of the Sphinx. Thus Oedipus's intelligence, a trait that brings Oedipus closer to the gods, is what also causes him to commit the most heinous of all possible sins. In killing the Sphinx, Oedipus is the city's savior, but in killing Laius (and marrying Jocasta), he is its scourge, the cause of the blight that has struck the city at the play's opening. Thus *Oedipus Rex* has been interpreted both as a warning against knowing more than one needs to know, and as a heroic testament to scientific investigation and truth-seeking. The play bears out both readings.

The Sphinx's riddle echoes throughout the play, even though Sophocles never quotes her actual question. Audiences familiar with the myth would have known the Sphinx's words: "What is it that goes on four feet in the morning, two feet at midday, and three feet in the evening?" Oedipus's answer, of course, was "a man." And in the course of the play, Oedipus himself proves to be that same man, an embodiment of the Sphinx's riddle. There is much talk of Oedipus's birth and his exposure as an infant - here is the baby of which the Sphinx speaks, forced, in this instance, to crawl on four feet as his ankles are pierced. Oedipus throughout most of the play is the adult man, standing on his own two feet instead of relying on others, even gods. And at the end of the play, Oedipus will leave Thebes an old blind man, using a cane. In fact, Oedipus's name means "swollen foot", presumably because of the pins thrust through his ankles as a baby. Oedipus is more than merely the solver of the Sphinx's riddle - he embodies its solution.

Perhaps the most significant example of dramatic irony in this play, however, involves the frequent reference to eyes, sight, light, and perception throughout. Oedipus, of course, cannot see behind him or in front of him. Unlike blind Teiresias, the seer, he is firmly located in the present. Accordingly, then, Teiresias, as he says early in the play, sees Oedipus as blind. The irony is that sight here means two different things. Oedipus is blessed with the gift of perception; he was the only man who could "see" the answer to the Sphinx's riddle. Yet he cannot see what is right before his eyes, blind to the truth, for all he seeks it. Teiresias's presence in the play, then, is doubly important. As a blind old man, he foreshadows Oedipus's own future, and the more Oedipus mocks his blindness, the more ironic he sounds to the audience. Teiresias is a man who understands the truth without the use of his sight; Oedipus is the opposite, a sighted man who is blind to the truth right before him. Soon Oedipus will switch roles with Teiresias, becoming a man who sees the truth and loses his sense of sight.

Teiresias is not the only character who uses sight as a metaphor. When Creon appears after learning of Oedipus's accusation of him, he asks “Were his eyes straight in his head?” (528). Yet Oedipus will be ashamed to look any who love him in the eyes. Indeed, one reason that he blinds himself is because he does not want to have to look on his father or mother in the afterlife. A number of binaries are associated with the idea of sight and blindness: illusion and disillusion, light and dark, morning and night. Time casts its searchlight at random, and when it does, it uncovers terrible things. The happiness of the "morning of light" is an illusion, while the reality is the "night of endless darkness." The Chorus, meanwhile, wishes it had never seen Oedipus. Not only has he polluted his own sight and his own body by marrying his mother and killing his father, he is a pollutant of others' sights by his very existence. When Oedipus enters, blinded, the Chorus tells him he has sprung to a terrible place “whereof men’s ears / may not hear, nor their eyes behold it” (1313-4). Oedipus has become the very blight he wishes to remove from Thebes, a monster more terrible than the Sphinx that must be cast out in order to save the kingdom.

Suggested Essay Questions

1. **Oedipus remains in the dark. Do you agree?**

   This question asks you to consider the importance of dark and light, and therefore perhaps also sight, in the play. Think metaphorically (i.e. 'in the dark' - unknowing) but also literally (Oedipus' blinding at the end of the play).
2. **Oedipus is old before his time. Do you agree?**

   This question asks you to consider question of youth and age in Oedipus - though the action of the play happens in a single day, how might Oedipus be considered old? You might also want to think about fathers and children and the impact generation has on age.
3. **This play happens backward. Do you agree?**

   This question asks you to consider the structure of the play. Look at the section on 'Myth' and consider the way Sophocles alters the story to turn it into a drama. What does Oedipus know at the start of the play? What does he know at the end? What events actually occur during the play - or have all the events happened before it begins?
4. **How might a consideration of the conditions of Greek theatrical performance impact upon our understanding of Oedipus Rex?**

   This question asks you to consider the importance of the Greek theatrical conventions (particularly masks) that would have originally been employed when Oedipus was performed. Think practically - there were no electric lights, no recorded music, and perhaps even no props. How might this change your interpretation of the play? (See 'About Greek Theater' for more information).
5. **Is *Oedipus Rex* a private or a public play?**

   This question asks you to consider the relationship between public and private (or between oikos/polis) in the play. What is the outcome for Thebes? What is the outcome for Oedipus? Is Oedipus to be considered as a father/son/brother or simply as the king of Thebes?
6. **Might Oedipus be more than one man?**

   This question asks you to consider the play's central inconsistency as potentially one of its themes. The Thebans have heard that Laius was killed by more than one man; in fact, Oedipus alone committed the murder. Think of Oedipus' various roles in the play - king/brother/father/son - and consider whether the conflict of the play might be a conflict between the one and the many.
7. **Do you agree that Oedipus' tragedy happens because of a 'tragic flaw'?**

This question asks you to consider that Oedipus' tragedy happens because of a tragic flaw - an opinion that many critics would strongly disagree with. Why do the events of the play happen? Whose fault is it - if anyone's? See *Oedipus and Aristotle* for more information about the idea of tragic flaws.

8. **"The old seer had eyes" (Oedipus the King, 748). Discuss ideas of sight and blindness in the play.**

   As well as thinking literally about blindness in Oedipus (Teiresias, in particular) consider the relationship between knowledge and sight. Does Oedipus have any insight into things - can he, perhaps, see better without his eyes?

9. **"I stumbled when I saw" (Gloucester, in Shakespeare's *King Lear*). Compare *Oedipus Rex* to any other play of your choice.**

   This question invites you to compare Oedipus to any other play. You might want to think about themes, about characters, or what you consider to be the ultimate lesson of the play - just remember to keep comparing: write about both plays at once, not one and then the other. See *Useful Comparison Points* for some good ideas.

10. **How does Oedipus come to embody the riddle of the Sphinx?**

    This question requires you to make a connection between the Sphinx riddle's answer - 'man' - and Oedipus' fate. Oedipus, as a consequence of seeking the answer to his kingdom's plague, manages to go through the three stages of the Sphinx's riddle. He is the baby with pierced ankles, crawling on four feet to escape a messenger who would kill him. Then he is the proud adult, king of Thebes, walking on two feet. And finally he is the old, blinded man, walking with a cane, cast out of his own kingdom.

The Oedipus Myth

You will often come across myth discussed alongside any of the Greek tragedies you study. This is simply because the Greeks tended to refer to myths for the source of plots for their plays, rather than to invent plots of their own or to dramatize real-life events (in fact, Phrynichus' play, *The Sack of Miletus*, got him a fine of 1000 drachmas for doing exactly that).

This is, perhaps, where the inevitability so often associated with Greek Tragedy stems from: many or most of the Athenian audience who first watched these plays at the City Dionysia and other dramatic festivals would be familiar with the **story** of Oedipus - and know what to expect as soon as they heard his name.

The story that they would have known is the same as that of Sophocles' play. What is compelling, however, is the way Sophocles chooses to dramatize it – the precise way he packages the well-known story into a play. The story of Oedipus itself is by no means Sophocles' invention, but he reorganizes the way the information is given so as to provide maximum tension.

The story of the myth is as follows – in chronological order:

The King of Thebes was Laius, a descendant of Cadmus, and an oracle predicted, before the birth of his son, that this son would one day be his father's murderer. When born, Laius (and, in some versions of the myth, Jocasta, Oedipus' mother and Laius' wife) gives the child to a herdsman and orders him to take him out beyond the city and kill him. Out of pity for the child, the herdsman gave the baby to another herdsman, tying his feet together and wounding them (in some versions, Laius pierces Oedipus' feet and exposes him to die, where the herdsman finds him by chance). This herdsman took the baby to Polybus, King of Corinth, who adopted him as his own son.

Oedipus, now fully grown, is told that he is not the son of Polybus, and seeks help from an oracle, who tells him he is destined to kill his father and sleep with his mother. Oedipus – presumably still thinking that Polybus is his father – flees from Corinth to Thebes in an attempt to escape the fate the oracle has predicted for him. As he is travelling, he gets involved in a dispute at a crossroads with a man in a chariot (Laius, his birth father) – and kills him.

As he approaches Thebes, Oedipus is approached by the Sphinx, who proposes her famous riddle: 'What walks on four feet in the morning, two in the afternoon, and three at night?' – the answer is man, who crawls, walks upright, and in his age, walks with a stick. The Sphinx, who has been plaguing Thebes, is defeated – Oedipus has solved the riddle that no Athenian could solve. In gratitude, the Thebans appoint Oedipus the king of Thebes (in Laius' place) and reward him with the dead king's wife, Jocasta, his birth mother. Oedipus and Jocasta have four children: two daughters (Electra and Ismene) and two sons (Polyneices and Eteocles).

At this point, Sophocles' play begins. Years later, a plague strikes Thebes, and Oedipus as King promises to end it. He sends Creon, Jocasta's brother, to the Delphic Oracle to seek guidance and is told that the murderer of Laius must be found and either killed or exiled (depending, again, on which version you read). As he begins to search for the killer, he encounters (or sends for) Tiresias, who tells him that he is the killer of Laius and warns him that he will only be seeking out himself. Oedipus ignores this advice.

A messenger arrives from Corinth giving Oedipus the news that Polybus is dead, and it seems the oracle's prophecy for Oedipus has failed to come true. The herdsman who delivered him to Corinth then appears and informs Oedipus that he is an adopted baby. Jocasta, hearing this, realizes what has happened and kills herself. Oedipus seeks out the herdsman initially ordered to murder him as a baby, and learns that the infant raised by Polybus and Merope (his wife) was in fact the son of Laius and Jocasta. He finally realizes that, at the crossroads, he killed his father, and is married to his own mother. Notably in Sophocles' play, the Corinthian Messenger is also the first herdsman: a small, but concise tweak.

Oedipus finds Jocasta dead, and blinds himself. He then (in Sophocles) leaves the city, and with his daughter Antigone as his guide, wanders blindly through the country, dying finally at Colonos. Some versions of the story have Oedipus commit suicide in Thebes, rather than leave or be exiled.

Oedipus and Aristotle

In his Poetics, Aristotle outlined the ingredients necessary for a good tragedy, and based his formula on what he considered to be the perfect tragedy, Sophocles's *Oedipus the King.* According to Aristotle, a tragedy must be an imitation of life in the form of a serious story that is complete in itself; in other words, the story must be realistic and narrow in focus.

A good tragedy will evoke pity and fear in its viewers, causing the viewers to experience a feeling of catharsis. Catharsis, in Greek, means "purgation" or "purification"; running through the gamut of these strong emotions will leave viewers feeling elated, in the same way we often claim that crying might ultimately make you feel better.

Aristotle also outlined the characteristics of an ideal tragic hero. He must be "better than we are," a man who is superior to the average man in some way. In Oedipus's case, he is superior not only because of social standing, but also because he is smart: he is the only person who could solve the Sphinx's riddle. At the same time, a tragic hero must evoke both pity and fear, and Aristotle claims that the best way to do this is if he is imperfect. A character with a mixture of good and evil is more compelling that a character who is merely good. And Oedipus is far from perfect; although a clever man, he is blind to the truth and stubbornly refuses to believe Teiresias's warnings. Although he is a good father, he unwittingly fathered children in incest. A tragic hero suffers because of his hamartia, a Greek word that is often mistakenly translated as "tragic flaw" but really means "mistake". Oedipus' mistake - killing his father at the crossroads - is made unknowingly. Indeed, for him, there is no way of escaping his fate.

The focus on fate reveals another aspect of a tragedy as outlined by Aristotle: dramatic irony. Good tragedies are crammed with irony. The audience knows the outcome of the story already, but the hero does not, making his actions seem painfully ignorant in the face of what is to come. Whenever a character attempts to change fate, this is ironic to an audience who knows that the tragic outcome of the story - as they know it in the myth - cannot be avoided.

Useful Comparison Points

If you are writing an essay about *Oedipus Rex*, it is worth referring to the huge influence that Sophocles' play has had upon later literature. Many, many plays, films and books have drawn upon the story of Oedipus, and some of them might make excellent comparison. A short, and by no means exhaustive, list of such works is below.

Aeschylus, The Oresteia (458 BC).

Seneca, Oedipus (first century CE).

Shakespeare, King Lear (c.1605).

Shakespeare, Hamlet (c.1600).

Shakespeare, Macbeth (c.1605).

Jean Cocteau, The Infernal Machine (1934).

Arthur Miller, All My Sons (1947).

Steven Berkoff, Greek (1980).

Edward Albee, The Goat (2002).

You should also read Sophocles' sequel to *Oedipus Rex*, composed at the very end of his life, *Oedipus at Colonos*.

You might also, for a more humorous perspective, look at Tom Lehrer's song Oedipus Rex (1959).

About Greek Theater

For the Greeks, the word 'tragedy' was used much as we use the word 'play' - but it does not carry the same implications of our modern word 'tragedy'.

In Athens, the performance of tragedies took place as part of festivals - the most famous being the City Dionysia, a festival which worshipped the god Dionysos. Dionysos is the god of wine, of revelry, of theatre, of frenzy and of ambiguity - a reading of Euripides *Bacchae* goes much of the way to explain some of the logic behind his association with the Greek theatre.

The price of a ticket to the festival was distributed by the deme (the local town council) to each citizen whose record was good, and the audience sat in the open-air theatre below the Akropolis, divided into the same ten wedge-shaped sections that they sat in for public meetings. It is extremely clear, therefore, that, in the words of Froma Zeitlin "theater attendance was thus closely linked to citizenship". The Athenian festivals, as well as celebrating Dionysos, were designed to celebrate Athenian democracy and the power of the polis.

The festivals sometimes lasted several days, and involved sacrifices, choral singing, the performances of comedies and religious rites as well as the tragedy competition; and one of the key things to understand about the importance of *agon* in Greek drama is that these tragedies were written to compete against other tragedies. Budding playwrights submitted three tragedies together (though not always – and, in most instances, rarely – thematically linked together) and a satyr play, and three playwrights were chosen to have their trilogies and satyr play performed in a competition. Ten judges, chosen by lots, would then vote for, respectively, the first, second and third prizes.

The Greek theatre itself was famously built with a fan-shaped auditorium, in what is now called an 'amphitheatre' layout. Modern examples of this layout include the Royal National Theater's Olivier auditorium, and a Greek theatre of this kind survives at Epidaurous (pictured). The stage was likely circular, and the back wall of the stage was probably a permanent stone building, the 'skene', in which costumes and props could be stored, and which served variously as the internal locations the play might require (houses, tents, etc.). The performances themselves would have included little or no props, and probably very minimal costumes. The actors probably doubled several roles between them (Sophocles famously used three actors for his plays) and differentiated between them by switching masks.

The Oedipus Complex

The Oedipus Complex is a psychoanalytical theory created by Sigmund Freud (pictured) and derived heavily from Sophocles' play. Influenced by Freud, many later critics (and forward to this day) find elements of the Oedipus Complex in the relationship between Hamlet and Gertrude.

The theory dictates that all children feel sexual desire for the parent of the opposite sex and the death of the parent of the same sex, and is today believed to be manifest only in very young children. In terms of the play, the Oedipus Complex is extremely unhelpful: firstly, because Oedipus is not a child when Sophocles' play takes place, but secondly (and more importantly) because the play rests on the fact that he is unaware of the identity of his parents when he respectively murders and sleeps with them.

Author of ClassicNote and Sources

Robert William, author of ClassicNote. Completed on April 30, 2008, copyright held by GradeSaver.

Updated and revised Soman Chainani April 30, 2008. Copyright held by GradeSaver.

Sophocles. Oedipus the King. (translated by David Grene) Chicago: The University of Chicago Press, 1991.

Sophocles. Oedipus the King. (translated by Hugh Lloyd-Jones) Harvard: Loeb Classical Library, 1994.

Simon Goldhill. Reading Greek Tragedy. Cambridge: Cambridge University Press, 1986.

Froma Zeitlin, and John J. Winkler. Nothing to Do with Dionysos?. Princeton, New Jersey: Princeton University Press, 1990.

John Drakakis and Naomi Conn Liebler. Tragedy. London and New York: Longman, 1998.

Bernard Knox (and others). Word and Action: Essays on the Ancient Theater. Baltimore and London: John Hopkins University Press, 1979.

H.D.F. Kitto. Greek Tragedy. London: Barnes and Noble, 1966.

Essay: Hubris in Antigone and Oedipus

by Braden Ruddy
July 24, 2002

The idea of hubris is monumental in a plethora of Greek mythological works. In many ways the excessive pride of certain characters fuels their own destruction. This is certainly true with respect to the characters of Pentheus, Antigone, and Oedipus. All three of these characters demonstrate, through their actions, various degrees of arrogance that seem to undercut the traditional role of the Gods, and thus largely contribute to their downfall. However, it should be noted that while each of these characters demonstrate hubris, they way in which their arrogance manifests itself is unique to each character.

Pentheus, the authoritarian newly appointed king of Thebes is immediately troubled with the rising influence and odd rituals that surround Dionysus. He seeks to prove his authority and influence over the kingdom, and crush the leader of these ecstatic rituals, which he perceives as a direct threat to his rule. Early on in the play Pentheus is warned by Tiresias, the old seer of the kingdom not to over stretch his bounds and to respect Dionysus as he would the other gods. "No we don[1]t play at theologians with the gods. We stay close to the hallowed tenets of our fathers, old as time. Nothing can undo them ever. I don[1]t care how brilliant or abstruse the reasons are" (Euripides 404). This passage is significant because it provides Pentheus with a direct warning not let his own pompous notions of earthly and temporal power go against the divine will of the gods. Pentheus disregards the warning and goes ahead in a direct act of sacrilege by destroying the sylvan alter and detains Dionysus. As Pentheus interrogates Dionysus he again is issued a direct warning not to go against the will of the gods by persecuting one whom the gods favor. As Dionysus calmly states, "Very well, I[1]ll go along with this wrongful undestined destiny, but remember this: Dionysus, who you say does not exist, will wreak revenge on you for this" (Euripides 417). The story culminates in Dionysus playing on Pentheus[1] curiosity and voyeurism regarding the intoxicated hordes of Thebian women, by tricking him to go out to see them in action. Pentheus is brutally ripped apart by the possessed women, yet in effect it was his own actions that caused his destruction. As Dionysus directly addresses the hubris of Pentheus, "The sins of jealousy and anger made this Pentheus deal unjustly with one bringing blessings, whom he disgracefully imprisoned and insulted; and so he met his end at the hands of his own kin an unnatural end and yet a just one" (Euripides 453).

Antigone also over steps her bounds, yet in a drastically different way. Rather than embracing the authoritarian ideals and decrees of Creon, the Stalinist new leader of Thebes, Antigone[1]s dual sense of pride and stubbornness fuels her personal reactions. Her belief that her brother deserves a proper burial seems to transcend logic and directly counter both temporal and divine authority. Antigone herself, by burying her brother, has taken on the role of the gods. Thus, she contributes to her own downfall. While Antigone believes that her actions are defending a moral good, it is the way in which she goes about her actions that propel her own hubris. She makes the burial rights a public question, rather than using tact and diplomacy to approach Creon as Haemon demonstrates. Both Antigone and Creon are wrapped up in a personal struggle that is quite stubborn. Her actions, like that of Creon¹s, are acts of hubris. The fact that Creon is wrong doesn¹t justify the actions of Antigone. In this respect both characters are quite similar despite their protagonist nature. As the chorus states, "Surpassing belief, the device and cunning that man has attained, and it bringeth him now to evil, now to good" (Sophocles 14).

Oedipus perhaps demonstrates the most direct and painfully obvious acts of hubris of the three characters. His temper plays a crucial role throughout the play, along with his arrogance. He possesses a precipitous rage in his blind quest to uncover his past. Again, his grandiose sense of pride and impulse ignites his destined downfall. From the onset, the vanity of Oedipus is latent when he travels, against warnings, to the oracle of Delphi. His inflated notions of his stature as ruler directly question the authority of the gods, and lead to his eventual decay. Oedipus represents common notions inherent in tragedies of the precarious sense of human prosperity. Oedipus, in an extremely short time, has extreme highs and lows, which demonstrate the classic patterns of the god¹s rough justice. This sudden and constantly altering nature of fate leads Oedipus to glory, yet his stubborn and arrogant quest to see¹ ultimately blinds him, as he is reduced to nothing in an instant. Oedipus¹ story exemplifies how destiny is inescapable. His quest to outwit fate, in effect, perpetuates his own destruction. This notion of tragic irony trying to run away from destiny yet perpetuating it instead, illustrates the hubris of Oedipus. By disregarding the knowledge and warnings of Teiresias, and thus the gods, Oedipus¹s stubborn sense of pride goes directly against the will of the gods. Ironically it is Oedipus who states, "True; but to force the gods against their will that is a thing beyond all power" (Sophocles 57). Simply put, Oedipus can not see that his actions are doing just that, and only when his hubris is punished and he losses his literal eyesight, can he finally see the truth.

Essay: Hubris in Greek Mythology

by Braden Ruddy
November 25, 2002

The idea of hubris is monumental in a plethora of Greek mythological works. In many ways the excessive pride of certain characters fuels their own destruction. This is certainly true with respect to the characters of Pentheus, Antigone, and Oedipus. All three of these characters demonstrate, through their actions, various degrees of arrogance that seem to undercut the traditional role of the Gods, and thus largely contribute to their downfall. However, it should be noted that while each of these characters demonstrate hubris, they way in which their arrogance manifests itself is unique to each character.

Pentheus, the authoritarian newly appointed king of Thebes is immediately troubled with the rising influence and odd rituals that surround Dionysus. He seeks to prove his authority and influence over the kingdom, and crush the leader of these ecstatic rituals, which he perceives as a direct threat to his rule. Early on in the play Pentheus is warned by Tiresias, the old seer of the kingdom not to over stretch his bounds and to respect Dionysus as he would the other gods. "No we don't play at theologians with the gods. We stay close to the hallowed tenets of our fathers, old as time. Nothing can undo them ever. I don't care how brilliant or abstruse the reasons are" (Euripides 404). This passage is significant because it provides Pentheus with a direct warning not let his own pompous notions of earthly and temporal power go against the divine will of the gods. Pentheus disregards the warning and goes ahead in a direct act of sacrilege by destroying the sylvan alter and detains Dionysus. As Pentheus interrogates Dionysus he again is issued a direct warning not to go against the will of the gods by persecuting one whom the gods favor. As Dionysus calmly states, "Very well, I'll go along with this wrongful undestined destiny, but remember this: Dionysus, who you say does not exist, will wreak revenge on you for this" (Euripides 417). The story culminates in Dionysus playing on Pentheus' curiosity and voyeurism regarding the intoxicated hordes of Thebian women, by tricking him to go out to see them in action. Pentheus is brutally ripped apart by the possessed women, yet in effect it was his own actions that caused his destruction. As Dionysus directly addresses the hubris of Pentheus, "The sins of jealousy and anger made this Pentheus deal unjustly with one bringing blessings, whom he disgracefully imprisoned and insulted; and so he met his end at the hands of his own kin an unnatural end and yet a just one" (Euripides 453).

Antigone also over steps her bounds, yet in a drastically different way. Rather than embracing the authoritarian ideals and decrees of Creon, the Stalinist new leader of Thebes, Antigone's dual sense of pride and stubbornness fuels her personal reactions. Her belief that her brother deserves a proper burial seems to transcend logic and directly counter both temporal and divine authority. Antigone herself, by burying her brother, has taken on the role of the gods. Thus, she contributes to her own downfall.

While Antigone believes that her actions are defending a moral good, it is the way in which she goes about her actions that propel her own hubris. She makes the burial rights a public question, rather than using tact and diplomacy to approach Creon as Haemon demonstrates. Both Antigone and Creon are wrapped up in a personal struggle that is quite stubborn. Her actions, like that of Creon's, are acts of hubris. The fact that Creon is wrong doesn't justify the actions of Antigone. In this respect both characters are quite similar despite their protagonist nature. As the chorus states, "Surpassing belief, the device and cunning that man has attained, and it bringeth him now to evil, now to good" (Sophocles 14).

Oedipus perhaps demonstrates the most direct and painfully obvious acts of hubris of the three characters. His temper plays a crucial role throughout the play, along with his arrogance. He possesses a precipitous rage in his blind quest to uncover his past. Again, his grandiose sense of pride and impulse ignites his destined downfall. From the onset, the vanity of Oedipus is latent when he travels, against warnings, to the oracle of Delphi. His inflated notions of his stature as ruler directly question the authority of the gods, and lead to his eventual decay. Oedipus represents common notions inherent in tragedies of the precarious sense of human prosperity. Oedipus, in an extremely short time, has extreme highs and lows, which demonstrate the classic patterns of the god's rough justice. This sudden and constantly altering nature of fate leads Oedipus to glory, yet his stubborn and arrogant quest to see' ultimately blinds him, as he is reduced to nothing in an instant. Oedipus' story exemplifies how destiny is inescapable. His quest to outwit fate, in effect, perpetuates his own destruction. This notion of tragic irony trying to run away from destiny yet perpetuating it instead, illustrates the hubris of Oedipus. By disregarding the knowledge and warnings of Teiresias, and thus the gods, Oedipus's stubborn sense of pride goes directly against the will of the gods. Ironically it is Oedipus who states, "True; but to force the gods against their will that is a thing beyond all power" (Sophocles 57). Simply put, Oedipus can not see that his actions are doing just that, and only when his hubris is punished and he losses his literal eyesight, can he finally see the truth.

Quiz 1

1. **What is the priest doing at the beginning of the play?**
   A. Asking the gods for help
   B. Accusing Oedipus
   C. Asking Teiresias for help
   D. Sacrificing to the Sphinx

2. **Why is the priest doing this?**
   A. There is a plague on the city
   B. The Sphinx has attacked the city
   C. It's a holiday
   D. Oedipus asked him to

3. **Where did Oedipus send Creon at the beginning of the play?**
   A. To the Pythian oracle
   B. To Delphi
   C. To Corinth
   D. To be banished from Thebes

4. **What does Creon report?**
   A. That he will kill his father and marry his mother
   B. That Teiresias killed Laius
   C. That Jocasta's son must be found
   D. That Laius's killer must be found

5. **What should happen to the man they will find?**
   A. He must be put in jail
   B. He must become the next king
   C. He must be sacrificed to the Sphinx
   D. He must be banished or killed

6. **Why didn't anyone investigate Laius's murder at the time?**
   A. There was a blight on the city
   B. They didn't want anyone to know that Oedipus did it
   C. Jocasta went into labor
   D. The Sphinx was attacking the city

7. **What does Oedipus announce to the Theban people?**
    A. That if any man confesses, he will only be banished
    B. That he too will be punished if he helps the killer
    C. That if anyone knows who killed Laius, he should come forward
    D. All of the above

8. **Who is rumored to have killed Laius?**
    A. Jocasta
    B. Robbers
    C. Teiresias
    D. All of the above

9. **Who does Creon advise Oedipus to send for?**
    A. Jocasta
    B. A shepherd
    C. Teiresias
    D. The sphinx

10. **What does Teiresias say when he arrives?**
    A. That the Sphinx did it
    B. That Creon did it
    C. That he will not tell who did it
    D. That Jocasta did it

11. **How does Oedipus respond when Teiresias charges him with killing Laius?**
    A. He calls Teiresias a blind fool
    B. He accuses Creon of killing Laius
    C. He accuses Teiresias of conspiring with Creon
    D. All of the above

12. **What does Teiresias say will happen to Oedipus?**
    A. He will marry Antigone
    B. He will leave Thebes in triumph
    C. He will leave Thebes a blind beggar
    D. He will kill himself

13. **What does Oedipus ask Creon?**
   A. Why Teiresias conspired with the Sphinx
   B. Why Teiresias is blind
   C. Why Jocasta married Laius
   D. Why Teiresias didn't say anything at the time of Laius's death

14. **Does Creon say he wants to be king?**
   A. No
   B. Only if Oedipus rules with him
   C. Yes
   D. Only if he can marry Jocasta

15. **What does Jocasta convince Oedipus to do to Creon?**
   A. Kill him
   B. Banish him
   C. Abandon him
   D. Forgive him

16. **What does Jocasta attempt to prove to Oedipus?**
   A. That there is no truth in prophesy
   B. That Teiresias is really his father
   C. That Creon killed Laius
   D. That the oracles are always right

17. **What does she say she did with her baby?**
   A. She gave it to her maid to raise
   B. She sacrificed it on the altar of Athena
   C. She drowned it in the well
   D. She left it exposed on a mountain

18. **Where was Laius killed?**
   A. At a crossroads
   B. In his bath
   C. At the battle of Troy
   D. In jail

19. **Why does Jocasta's story upset Oedipus?**
   A. He was a witness to this death
   B. He killed a man at a crossroads
   C. He fought at Troy
   D. His father was killed in a similar way

20. **What made Oedipus go to the oracle when he was young?**
   A. Teiresias told him to
   B. Creon tried to kill him
   C. His parents told him to
   D. A man called him a bastard

21. **What did the oracle tell Oedipus?**
   A. That his mother was Jocasta
   B. That he should stay away from Thebes
   C. That he would kill his father and marry his mother
   D. That he would become blind

22. **Why did Oedipus leave Corinth?**
   A. He wanted to find his real dad
   B. He was afraid of what the oracle said
   C. He was angry at the oracle
   D. He was summoned to kill the Sphinx

23. **What is Jocasta doing the next time she leaves the palace?**
   A. Killing her children
   B. Burying evidence
   C. Running away from Thebes
   D. Praying to the gods

24. **What news does the messenger bring from Corinth?**
   A. That Polybus was not Oedipus's father
   B. That Polybus is dead
   C. That Corinth wants Oedipus to be its king
   D. All of the above

25. **Who gave Oedipus to Polybus and Merope?**

A. The messenger

B. Jocasta

C. The Sphinx

D. Teiresias

Quiz 1 Answer Key

1. (**A**) Asking the gods for help
2. (**A**) There is a plague on the city
3. (**A**) To the Pythian oracle
4. (**D**) That Laius's killer must be found
5. (**D**) He must be banished or killed
6. (**D**) The Sphinx was attacking the city
7. (**D**) All of the above
8. (**B**) Robbers
9. (**C**) Teiresias
10. (**C**) That he will not tell who did it
11. (**D**) All of the above
12. (**C**) He will leave Thebes a blind beggar
13. (**D**) Why Teiresias didn't say anything at the time of Laius's death
14. (**A**) No
15. (**D**) Forgive him
16. (**A**) That there is no truth in prophesy
17. (**D**) She left it exposed on a mountain
18. (**A**) At a crossroads
19. (**B**) He killed a man at a crossroads
20. (**D**) A man called him a bastard
21. (**C**) That he would kill his father and marry his mother
22. (**B**) He was afraid of what the oracle said
23. (**D**) Praying to the gods
24. (**D**) All of the above
25. (**A**) The messenger

Quiz 2

1. **Where did this person get Oedipus?**
   A. From a servant of Laius's household
   B. From Teiresias
   C. From Jocasta
   D. From Polybus

2. **How does Jocasta respond to the messenger's story?**
   A. She begs the messenger to continue
   B. She stabs the messenger
   C. She begs Oedipus to stop his line of questions
   D. She rejoices that the truth has come out

3. **Why does Oedipus think she does this?**
   A. She is afraid that Teiresias will kill him
   B. She is afraid that Oedipus is her son
   C. She is afraid he is only a peasant
   D. She is afraid that he will kill her

4. **What does the shepherd say when he arrives?**
   A. He doesn't want to tell
   B. He doesn't remember
   C. He never saw the messenger before
   D. All of the above

5. **How does Oedipus treat this shepherd?**
   A. He hugs and kisses him
   B. He banishes him
   C. He physically threatens him
   D. He kills him

6. **Where does the shepherd say the baby was from?**
   A. A peasant house
   B. The shepherd's own house
   C. Laius's household
   D. The temple of Apollo

7. **Who gave the baby to the shepherd?**
   A. Jocasta
   B. Polybus
   C. The Sphinx
   D. Laius

8. **Where does Oedipus go when he hears this news?**
   A. Back to Corinth
   B. Into the palace
   C. Away from the city
   D. Into the temple of Apollo

9. **What did Jocasta do when she ran into the house?**
   A. Drown herself
   B. Stab her children
   C. Hang herself
   D. Stab herself

10. **What did Oedipus do when he first ran into the house?**
   A. Grabbed his children
   B. Killed Jocasta
   C. Killed Creon
   D. Grabbed a sword and searched for Jocasta

11. **What does Oedipus gouge his eyes out with?**
   A. A dagger
   B. His sword
   C. His medal of honor
   D. Jocasta's brooches

12. **Why did Oedipus do this?**
   A. He couldn't bear to look at his father in the underworld
   B. He didn't want sight when all he saw was ugly
   C. He couldn't bear to look at Jocasta in the underworld
   D. All of the above

13. **How does Creon treat Oedipus?**
   A. He banishes him
   B. He is kind to him
   C. He is angry with him
   D. He gloats over his victory

14. **What does Oedipus want to do?**
   A. Kill Creon
   B. Kill his children
   C. Leave Thebes
   D. Kill himself

15. **Why doesn't Creon let him leave immediately?**
   A. He has to bury Jocasta
   B. He has to wait for Apollo's word
   C. He has to kill Teiresias
   D. He has to take care of his children

16. **Where does the play open?**
   A. In front of the palace of Oedipus at Thebes
   B. In front of the palace of Oedipus at Corinth
   C. Inside Oedipus' palace at Thebes
   D. Inside Oedipus' palace at Corinth

17. **Who is on stage at the play's opening?**
   A. Oedipus alone
   B. A priest, the chorus and a crowd of children
   C. Oedipus and Jocasta
   D. A priest and Oedipus

18. **Who is Oedipus' real mother?**
   A. Merope
   B. Electra
   C. Jocasta
   D. Iphigenia

19. **Who is Oedipus' real father?**
   A. Polybus
   B. Teiresias
   C. Creon
   D. Laius

20. **What are the names of Oedipus' two sons?**
   A. Eteocles and Polyneices
   B. Creon and Antigone
   C. Antigone and Ismene
   D. Teiresias and Creon

21. **Which play continues Oedipus' story?**
   A. Electra
   B. Iphigenia at Aulis
   C. Oedipus at Colonus
   D. Philoctetes

22. **Oedipus is wounded...**
   A. in the face
   B. in the back
   C. in the thigh
   D. in the ankles

23. **What are the names of Oedipus' two daughters?**
   A. Electra and Antigone
   B. Antigone and Jocasta
   C. Electra and Ismene
   D. Antigone and Ismene

24. **Which other playwright supposedly wrote a version of the Oedipus story?**
   A. Euripides
   B. Aeschylus
   C. Meliffoles
   D. Shakespeare

25. **From what is Thebes suffering at the beginning of the play?**

A. A plague

B. A thunderstorm

C. A drought

D. A flood

Quiz 2 Answer Key

1. **(A)** From a servant of Laius's household
2. **(C)** She begs Oedipus to stop his line of questions
3. **(C)** She is afraid he is only a peasant
4. **(D)** All of the above
5. **(C)** He physically threatens him
6. **(C)** Laius's household
7. **(A)** Jocasta
8. **(B)** Into the palace
9. **(C)** Hang herself
10. **(D)** Grabbed a sword and searched for Jocasta
11. **(D)** Jocasta's brooches
12. **(D)** All of the above
13. **(B)** He is kind to him
14. **(C)** Leave Thebes
15. **(B)** He has to wait for Apollo's word
16. **(A)** In front of the palace of Oedipus at Thebes
17. **(B)** A priest, the chorus and a crowd of children
18. **(C)** Jocasta
19. **(D)** Laius
20. **(A)** Eteocles and Polyneices
21. **(C)** Oedipus at Colonus
22. **(D)** in the ankles
23. **(D)** Antigone and Ismene
24. **(B)** Aeschylus
25. **(A)** A plague

Quiz 3

1. **Oedipus was first performed at the...**
   A. City Dionysia
   B. Maidenhead Arts Centre
   C. National Greek Dramatic Competition
   D. City Theban

2. **The Theban Plays are...**
   A. a trilogy as performed, but not chronologically within the text
   B. four plays
   C. a trilogy chronologically, but written at different times
   D. not, in fact, a trilogy at all

3. **In classical times, Thebes was considered**
   A. the opposite - the Other - version of Athens
   B. an ideal of democracy
   C. a plague-pit
   D. a mythical city that didn't really exist

4. **Laius was the king of**
   A. Thebes
   B. Athens
   C. Corinth
   D. Greece

5. **The alternative title of Oedipus Rex is...**
   A. The story of Oedipus
   B. The Oedipus myth
   C. Oedipus Tyrannus
   D. Oedipus at Colonus

6. **Sophocles...**
   A. invented the Oedipus story
   B. took the story of Oedipus from myth
   C. received the Oedipus story in a dream from the gods
   D. stole the Oedipus story from an ancient book

7. **Teiresias is**
   A. German
   B. extremely young
   C. an expert in the Bacchanal
   D. blind

8. **Teiresias enters**
   A. with blood dripping from his eyes
   B. dancing
   C. led by a small boy
   D. carrying a statue

9. **Creon is...**
   A. Oedipus' brother
   B. Jocasta's brother
   C. married to his own mother
   D. the murderer of his father

10. **Laius was killed by...**
   A. several men, at a crossroads
   B. his wife
   C. his brother, who poured poison into his ear
   D. Oedipus, at a crossroads

11. **The state of Thebes is often compared to**
   A. A river
   B. A spaceship
   C. A ship
   D. A field

12. **When Oedipus has discovered what he has done...**
   A. he kill himself
   B. he strips naked
   C. he runs screaming from Thebes
   D. he blinds himself

13. **Laius was the son of**
   A. Jocasta
   B. Oedipus
   C. Labdacus
   D. Creon

14. **The play as a whole might be described as**
   A. any of the above
   B. a play obsessed with origins
   C. a detective story
   D. a classical tragedy

15. **Teiresias can see...**
   A. the next year
   B. the next month
   C. the future
   D. the next week

16. **Teiresias sees the future courtesy of the....**
   A. goddess Athena
   B. goddess Alcione
   C. god Apollo
   D. god Bacchae

17. **The City Dionysia was**
   A. the first recorded kareoke competition
   B. a religious festival
   C. a theatrical festival
   D. both a religious festival and a theatrical one

18. **The Chorus in this play are**
   A. Theban elders
   B. Theban youths
   C. ballerinas
   D. a group of children

19. **The Chorus would likely have been played by**
   A. old men
   B. young or teenaged boys
   C. old women
   D. girls

20. **Were women allowed on the Athenian stage?**
   A. No
   B. Only on weekdays
   C. Yes
   D. No-one is sure.

21. **Oedipus dies**
   A. at the end of the play
   B. twice during the play
   C. halfway through the play
   D. in a later play, Oedipus at Colonos

22. **Jocasta thinks that the baby Oedipus**
   A. was killed by exposure
   B. is now the king of Thebes
   C. was given to the king of Corinth
   D. was drowned

23. **When Jocasta realizes what has happened...**
   A. she commits suicide
   B. she cries out for Laius
   C. she is delighted
   D. she makes a long speech cursing Oedipus

24. **Which number is important in the play?**
   A. 2
   B. 5
   C. 7
   D. 38

25. **Freud famously invented**

A. a Creon complex

B. an Jocasta complex

C. an Oedipus complex

D. an Antigone complex

Quiz 3 Answer Key

1. **(A)** City Dionysia
2. **(D)** not, in fact, a trilogy at all
3. **(A)** the opposite - the Other - version of Athens
4. **(A)** Thebes
5. **(C)** Oedipus Tyrannus
6. **(B)** took the story of Oedipus from myth
7. **(D)** blind
8. **(C)** led by a small boy
9. **(B)** Jocasta's brother
10. **(D)** Oedipus, at a crossroads
11. **(C)** A ship
12. **(D)** he blinds himself
13. **(C)** Labdacus
14. **(A)** any of the above
15. **(C)** the future
16. **(C)** god Apollo
17. **(D)** both a religious festival and a theatrical one
18. **(A)** Theban elders
19. **(B)** young or teenaged boys
20. **(D)** No-one is sure.
21. **(D)** in a later play, Oedipus at Colonos
22. **(A)** was killed by exposure
23. **(A)** she commits suicide
24. **(A)** 2
25. **(C)** an Oedipus complex

Quiz 4

1. **The name for the 'building' structure on the Greek stage is**
   A. the skene
   B. the oikos
   C. the polis
   D. the palace

2. **The correct translation of the Greek "hamartia" is**
   A. a murder
   B. a mistake
   C. a flaw
   D. a tragic flaw

3. **Aristotle claimed that tragedies should evoke...**
   A. just laughter
   B. just tears
   C. laughter and tears
   D. pity and fear

4. **Aristotle believed Oedipus Rex was...**
   A. a model tragedy
   B. - he never read it
   C. the worst tragedy ever written
   D. a reasonably good tragedy

5. **Jocasta dies...**
   A. inside the palace
   B. in a forest
   C. outside the palace, on the steps
   D. on the beach

6. **Jocasta kills herself**
   A. by drowning herself
   B. by shooting herself
   C. by hanging herself
   D. with poison

7. **Oedipus was turned into a French play by**
   A. Cocteau
   B. Chekhov
   C. Ibsen
   D. Gogol

8. **Oedipus was transferred to 1980s Britain in...**
   A. Seneca's play 'Oedipus'
   B. Margaret Thatcher's autobiography
   C. Jean Cocteau's play 'The Infernal Machine'
   D. Steven Berkoff's play Greek

9. **At the end of the play, the Chorus say that**
   A. happiness is never safe from change
   B. everyone is sad
   C. they don't understand what's happened
   D. they feel very sorry for Oedipus

10. **Jocasta at one points enters**
   A. with a noose around her neck
   B. blinded
   C. with a loaded gun
   D. with garlands and incense for the gods

11. **Does Oedipus ever know his real parents?**
   A. No
   B. Yes but he never realizes his crimes
   C. Yes, and he realizes his crimes
   D. He knows them from the start of the play

12. **Polybus dies**
   A. drowning
   B. in a sinking ship
   C. of shock at what his son has done
   D. of sickness

13. **Sophocles wrote the Theban plays in this order:**
    A. Antigone, Oedipus the King, Oedipus at Colonos
    B. Oedipus the King, Oedipus at Colonus, Antigone
    C. Antigone, Oedipus at Colonos, Oedipus the King
    D. Oedipus the King, Antigone, Oedipus at Colonos

14. **Oedipus runs away from**
    A. Thebes
    B. Athens
    C. Corinth
    D. Greece

15. **Does Oedipus solve the riddle of the Sphinx?**
    A. No
    B. He refuses to answer it
    C. Yes
    D. He dies before it is solved

16. **The answer to the Sphinx's riddle is**
    A. Everyone
    B. Oedipus himself
    C. Man
    D. Woman

17. **The Sphinx has been terrorising**
    A. Thebes
    B. Athens
    C. Corinth
    D. Greece

18. **Oedipus was first performed in**
    A. Thebes
    B. Athens
    C. Corinth
    D. Greece

19. **At the end of the play, Thebes**
  A. is on fire
  B. is freed from the plague
  C. is defeated in a war
  D. falls under the sea

20. **How many shepherds are there in the play?**
  A. Two
  B. Five
  C. Nine
  D. Forty

21. **Which of the below is a central theme of the play?**
  A. Dancing
  B. Hearing
  C. Walking
  D. Sight

22. **Oedipus' name means**
  A. King of Thebes
  B. swollen-footed
  C. fat-faced
  D. murderer

23. **What crimes does Oedipus commit?**
  A. Kills his father, and sleeps with his mother
  B. Sleeps with his daughters and kills his sons
  C. Strangles his wife
  D. Murders his family

24. **Oedipus' final entrance into the play comes**
  A. from the wings
  B. across the roof of the skene building
  C. from within the palace - blinded
  D. as a deus ex machina

25. **The daughter who will later be Oedipus' guide is**

A. Ismene

B. Jocasta

C. Antigone

D. Creon

Quiz 4 Answer Key

1. (**A**) the skene
2. (**B**) a mistake
3. (**D**) pity and fear
4. (**A**) a model tragedy
5. (**A**) inside the palace
6. (**C**) by hanging herself
7. (**A**) Cocteau
8. (**D**) Steven Berkoff's play Greek
9. (**A**) happiness is never safe from change
10. (**D**) with garlands and incense for the gods
11. (**C**) Yes, and he realizes his crimes
12. (**D**) of sickness
13. (**A**) Antigone, Oedipus the King, Oedipus at Colonos
14. (**C**) Corinth
15. (**C**) Yes
16. (**C**) Man
17. (**A**) Thebes
18. (**B**) Athens
19. (**B**) is freed from the plague
20. (**A**) Two
21. (**D**) Sight
22. (**B**) swollen-footed
23. (**A**) Kills his father, and sleeps with his mother
24. (**C**) from within the palace - blinded
25. (**C**) Antigone

Made in the USA
Lexington, KY
02 January 2012